tabletop
fountains

tabletop
fountains

Rod Ferring

BARRON'S

First edition for the United States and Canada published in 2001 by Barron's Educational Series, Inc.

First published in 2001 by Interpet Publishing.
© Copyright 2001 by Interpet Publishing.

All inquiries should be addressed to:
Barron's Educational Series, Inc.
250 Wireless Boulevard
Hauppauge, NY 11788
http://www.barronseduc.com

International Standard Book No. 0-7641-1844-7

Library of Congress Catalog Card No. 2001091358

THE AUTHOR
Rod Ferring is an artist and modelmaker who has many years of experience in the professional graphics industry. He lives on the coast of West Sussex in England.

Acknowledgments
The publishers would like to thank the following people for their valuable help and advice during the preparation of this book: Ken McIntyre and Marco Rubano at Eureka International, Worthing, West Sussex for the generous loan of equipment.

Printed in China
9 8 7 6 5 4 3 2

contents

introduction 6

electrical essentials 8

materials and decorations 10

basic techniques 12

terracotta pot fountain 14

seashells and stones 16

chinese pavilion 18

bonsai garden 20

shishi-odoshi 22

midnight grotto 24

alpine stream 26

desert oasis 28

mediterranean courtyard 30

copper and slate waterfall 32

34 helter skelter

38 bamboo watersteps

40 glowing pyramid

42 scallop shell cascade

44 fragrant waterfall

46 water wheel

50 floating garden

52 double bubble

54 copper cascade

56 seashell shower

58 candlewall canals

60 miniature wall mask

62 tipping beak fountain

64 index

introduction

Anyone who walks through a garden center or a craft fair cannot fail to notice that a new fashion in home decoration is alive and kicking. Tabletop fountains greet the eye at every turn – water wheels spin, foggers breathe out mist, marble spheres spin silently on their plinths, water trickles from spouts and bowls, and bamboo deer-scarers duck their heads. People have realized that you do not need a garden or terrace to enjoy a water feature. By scaling everything down, the pleasure of a fountain or waterfall can be enjoyed inside the house, on a simple tabletop.

The key to this has been the development of small submersible pumps, lights, and misters that require practically no maintenance and are reliable enough to run for months without problem. But you do not necessarily have to make do with a fountain from off the shelf. The commercial availability of these items makes it possible for anyone to build a tabletop fountain of their own design at home, incorporating other materials that may be collected on a day out in the country or a browse through a second-hand shop. This book shows you exactly how to go about doing it.

The beneficial effects of introducing a tabletop fountain into the home are not simply aesthetic ones. The gentle sound of water induces a feeling of relaxation while some fountains also incorporate aromatherapy oils and candles to help soothe frayed nerves. Fountains can even de-stress your life.

Left: This simple arrangement features a small jug which pours a stream of water over the stones as long as the power is on and the bowl is filled with water. The pump is hidden from sight in the bottom of the jug.

Right: This Oriental-style fountain is conceived on a grander scale. Water trickles over the face of the volcanic stone while a mister concealed in the rockwork delivers clouds of fog that swirl down the gullies. The reservoir dish is hidden in the base of the fountain.

electrical essentials

There is one piece of equipment that is vital to any tabletop water feature – the electric pump that powers the whole creation. Without a pump, there can be no moving streams, tumbling fountains, or sounds of trickling water. So you must be prepared to invest in one of these before you can go any further. Fortunately they are not particularly expensive and they are normally quite reliable, so your initial outlay should buy many months or even years of trouble-free operation.

In recent years pump technology has improved. Small pumps are now available that are robust and powerful for their size. The secret has been the development of mag-drive or induction motors. These are magnet-driven devices – a magnet is attached to the impeller rotor that is the only moving part in the assembly. The motion of the rotor is not caused by a direct connection to the electric motor but rather by the interaction of the magnetic fields generated by the motor and the impeller magnet. The rotor and bearings

Above: *A mister in action. The plate that transmits the ultrasonic waves is set in the top. The snorkel device to the left of the unit is the water sensor. If the level of the water drops below this, the mister will stop running.*

are lubricated and cooled by the water, while the motor itself is housed in a waterproofed, sealed housing. This helps to eliminate water damage to the motor, while making it easy to take apart and clean the impeller and plastic filter casing of the pump.

Some pumps are also supplied with an integral halogen light as part of the unit. This requires the current to be stepped down, usually to 12 volts, and a

Above: *This is a small submersible pump that can be used to power a tabletop water feature. The output from the pump can usually be regulated by a flow control valve.*

Cleaning the Pump: *Modern mag-drive pumps require little in the way of maintenance. However, performance will be adversely affected if any grit or dirt are sucked into the unit. Remember to disassemble the pump on a regular basis and to scrub all the detachable components with a non-abrasive brush and then rinse them under clean running water.*

If you live in an area of hard water, the build-up of limescale in the pump can also pose a problem. Try leaving the affected parts soaking in lemon juice or vinegar – the acid naturally present in these liquids should dissolve the limescale. Then rinse the parts in clean water and reassemble the pump.

Misters – a Word of Warning: *Misters create a marvelous effect, but remember that the clouds of water vapor will eventually condense on surrounding surfaces. It makes sense to try out your fog feature in a place where stray drops of water will not do any damage before deciding on the final position of the fountain. Valuable items of furniture can be damaged by unwanted water spills.*

transformer is supplied for this purpose. The lamp is covered by a protective glass shade. Take care when handling the light if it has been illuminated for any time – it may still be hot to touch.

One other electrical device that can make an enormous difference to the visual character of a tabletop feature is the mister or fogger. This is small metal-cased unit that is submerged to a depth of about 2-4 in (5-10 cm) in water. It works by using ultrasonic sound waves that are transmitted via a transducer plate or ceramic membrane. These waves atomize the water above the plate and create swathes of water vapor on the surface which drift over the edge of the tabletop feature. A sensor unit detects the presence of water – if the level of the bowl drops below the sensor, which

may happen after time as the fogger consumes quite a lot of water when it is running, the sensor will turn the device off. Splash guards are also available to prevent droplets of water from shooting out in all directions. The performance of the mister can deteriorate after some months because of the build-up of mineral deposits on the plate. It is quite easy to remove it – a key simply unscrews a retaining ring – and the component can either be cleaned or replaced.

Safety: *Electricity and water make a potentially dangerous combination, so you must observe certain rules when assembling and adjusting tabletop fountains.*
• Always make sure that any electrical components connected to the power supply are protected by residual current circuit breakers.
• Disconnect all electrical appliances before putting your hands into the water to adjust the set-up or to take any units out of the water.
• Check that the voltage shown on the label of any unit matches the voltage of your power supply.
• Take care not to touch the lamp after it has been illuminated until it has had time to cool down.

Above: *A mister works off a transformer which typically steps the voltage down to 24V. The mister needs to be fully immersed in water to function properly.*

Above: *Seen here are a submersible pump and a combined pump and light unit. The impeller rotor and the flow control valve can be seen in the expanded view.*

Above: *Modern pumps are so compact that they can be concealed inside components of a display. Here a pump is being sealed inside the jug illustrated on page 6.*

materials and decorations

On these two pages we turn our attention to some of the other elements that are used to build a tabletop fountain. The first of these is the bowl in which the display sits and which holds the necessary water. It is also sometimes called the reservoir or sump. All sorts of choices are available: terracotta and ceramic pots, metal bowls and pans, plastic dishes, glass basins, the choice is vast. But remember that you do not have to buy a ready-made reservoir; with a little ingenuity almost any suitably shaped container can be turned into a perfectly acceptable sump. There are many types of spray paints available that brighten up virtually any surface, while silicone sealant is the ideal material to seal any holes or leaky seams to ensure a waterproof finish. Be careful, however, if you decide to use a porous material like terracotta; if the inside surface is not glazed, water can seep through the clay and cause a water stain on the surface of any wooden furniture.

The pipework that carries the water from the pump to the fountain outlet is normally made of clear plastic tubing. This is available in various gauges so you can match the internal diameter of the tube to the external diameter of any nozzle or outlet pipe that you need to. The tubing can also be sleeved together by sliding the end of a narrow-bore section of tube into a piece of slightly greater diameter. This enables you to

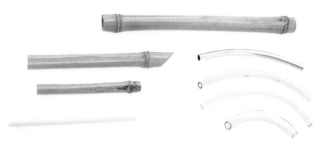

Above: *Pipework can be made from many materials, such as different gauges of bamboo and flexible plastic tubing, copper micro-bore pipe, and rigid plastic tubing.*

Left: *Don't assume that a tabletop fountain has to sit in a conventional bowl. Reservoirs can be round or oblong, shallow or deep – it all depends on what you want to create.*

link units with inlets and outlets of different gauge. Other options for pipework that you will see used in this book are rigid plastic piping, small-bore copper pipes, and bored-out sections of bamboo. All have good qualities and you will find more details about how and when to use them in the Projects section of the book.

Water and rocks naturally complement one another – you need only think of a rocky seascape or a stream tumbling down a mountainside to appreciate that. So the bowl of a fountain feature can look wonderful when decorated with an appropriate choice of stones, gravel,

Above: A big advantage of using mounting board, polystyrene or foamboard is that they all cut easily with a penknife or craft knife and are light to handle.

Above: Some of the enormous selection of stones, pebbles, gravel, and beads that await the fountain builder.

Above: Some of the artificial flowers, foliage, and wood that are available to decorate a fountain. Real flowers tend to fade too quickly to be a viable option.

or glass beads. The photograph opposite shows a small selection of the options available to you. Some you can buy from your local home store or garden center; others you may pick up on a walk in the country or a trip to the beach. The element of serendipity involved in collecting your materials is part of the fun of creating these features.

Some of the representational fountains illustrated in the book require you to build structures to mimic the look of buildings or to create regular symmetrical shapes for their visual effect. I have used various materials to do this, particularly mounting board, polystyrene, and foamboard. All of them are easy to handle and can be shaped precisely with a sharp penknife or craft knife. But remember that these are suggestions, not injunctions! If you want to use more durable materials, such as wood, plastic, or metal, feel free to do so.

Warning: *Remember that lit candles pose a fire hazard if they are not used responsibly. Never leave burning candles unattended, and position the fountain out of drafts and away from curtains or other materials that might blow into the flame and ignite. Take care when handling or extinguishing candles and nightlights – they may still be hot.*

basic techniques

Although the design of each tabletop fountain is unique and the construction of it requires you to solve a number of individual design problems, you will find that certain basic techniques underlie the construction of all the projects illustrated in this book. If you know how to assemble pipework and fountain outlets from rigid tubing, how to work with bamboo, how to introduce a controlled leak to reduce water flow, then soon you will have a basic armory of skills at your disposal that can be applied to a host of different water features.

Bamboo is an excellent material to work with. It is durable, rigid, and available in a variety of sizes or "gauges." It cuts easily and accurately, provided you use a sharp saw. A coat of clear varnish produces a marvellously glossy finish. It also has the great advantage that it is naturally hollow. Yes, the stems are blocked at the nodes where the leaf stems grow, but these blanking pieces actually work to the advantage of

1 *Flexible plastic tube comes in various bores or gauges. You will be able to find a size to fit your pump outlet and virtually any size of fountainhead.*

2 *If you need to connect elements that are of a different diameter, it is simple to slip the narrow-gauge pipe into the larger one to make a tight fit.*

the fountain maker. They mean that you can drill out a channel to carry water as far as you want it to go, but you have a natural barrier if you want to restrict the flow of water beyond a certain point. As you will see in the *Shishi-Odoshi* illustrated on pages 22-23, this

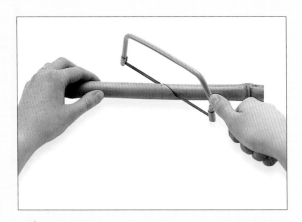

1 *To make a miter joint in a piece of bamboo, cut carefully through the length of wood at an angle of 45° as illustrated. Take care with this angle if you want to make a 90° spout.*

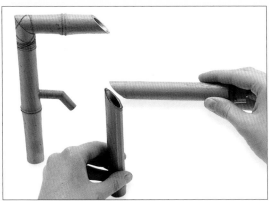

2 *Now reverse one piece of bamboo and assemble the joint as shown. The wood should be glued together with waterproof adhesive. You can use gold thread for extra decoration.*

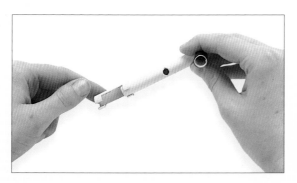

1 *To make a homemade shutter valve, take a piece of rigid plastic pipe, cut out a rectangular section with a hacksaw and then cut the two end sections longitudinally as shown.*

2 *You will now be able to slip this sleeve over your water delivery pipe. If you bore a hole in this to make a deliberate leak, you can regulate the flow rate by rotating the sleeve.*

characteristic of bamboo enables you to create a fountainhead that tips up and down as it fills with water and then empties itself in a cycle that repeats as long as the pump is running.

It is sometimes necessary to turn a rigid pipe 90° to create a horizontal cross-piece or a vertical downpipe. It is easy to do this by making a miter joint. You simply cut through a straight section of pipe at an angle of 45°, and then reverse one section of the pipe and glue the two angled faces together so that one piece of the pipe now projects at 90° from the other.

Electrical pumps are equipped with flow regulators that allow you to adjust the power of the jet of water emitted by the pump. They are usually simple fan-shaped pieces of plastic set in a ring that can be rotated to open or close the aperture through which the water flows. However, some fountains require very fine-tuning to create the right effect and the flow regulator may not be sensitive enough to allow you to find the right balance. The answer here is to introduce a controlled leak in the pipework. This can either be a small hole pierced in the tube, or a shutter arrangement such as the one illustrated which can be spun around to alter the size of the escape hole. Remember to site the

Above: *When polystyrene is used in the bottom of the reservoir, it will need weighing down with stones as ballast to prevent it from floating up on the water.*

hole in the right place so that the leak pours back into the reservoir and not out of the bowl onto the table!

Several of the projects in this book use polystyrene as a baseboard into which components such as the pump are fitted. It's a useful material because it is light, simple to cut, and it is easy to drive retaining pins into it to hold things firmly in position. Remember, however, that it does float, so if you plan to place it in the bottom of the bowl, you will have to use stones as ballast to weigh it down.

terracotta pot fountain

The first project in this book is deliberately a very simple arrangement that features a classic terracotta pitcher lying on its side in a shallow dish. From the mouth of the pitcher flows a stream of clear water which falls onto pebbles sited in the dish. A small pump concealed beneath the pitcher recycles the water from the reservoir or sump through a flexible tube into the body of the pitcher where it runs out of the mouth of the jar again. This is a straightforward arrangement to set up, and one that allows the beginner to experience the pleasure of making a small water feature at home very quickly. It also introduces you to the essential principles of creating tabletop fountains which underpin all the more complex creations that you will discover later in the book.

Essentially a tabletop feature uses a reservoir of water in which a small, electrical pump is situated to propel water to the desired outlet from where it flows down over the feature and drains back into the reservoir. All sorts of variations can be played on this theme, and various extra devices like lights, misters, and fountainheads added to the set-up, but the basic configuration of reservoir, pump, pipework and water outlet will be a constant feature throughout the book. It is the skeleton which you can flesh out in countless ways – just let your imagination take flight.

construction

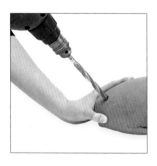

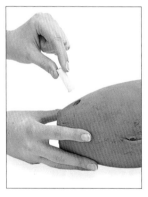

1 *A hole first needs to be drilled in the terracotta pot to allow a plastic tube to be pushed through it. This will be connected to the pump that is sited in the reservoir bowl below the pot. Terracotta drills fairly easily but it helps if you make a small pilot hole with a bradawl to guide the drill bit.*

2 *Once the hole has been drilled, insert a short length of rigid tubing though the aperture. This can be fixed in position with silicone sealant to ensure that the pot does not leak, but if the pipe naturally makes a tight fit without any sealant, don't worry – a little seepage is not serious.*

3 *The next step is to attach a short piece of flexible rubber tube to the outlet of the pump. The rigid pipe that you have just positioned in the pot will fit on to this when you assemble the fountain.*

4 *Now place a flat tile in the base of the reservoir bowl and press the pump firmly into position. The pump illustrated has small rubber suction cups for feet and these help to secure it in place and prevent it from slipping around and making unwanted movements when it is running.*

5 *The base of the reservoir is decorated with a selection of large pebbles. These also help to keep the pump in position.*

6 *Now the terracotta pot can be connected to the pump. Note how the white plastic tube attaches to the rubber collar that has been fitted to the pump's outlet pipe.*

7 *Finally twist the pot so that it sits comfortably on the stones in the bowl. A little gravel can be spooned inside the pot to conceal the plastic pipe and to form a visual link with the pebbles. Fill the bowl with water and turn on.*

The finished fountain running gently. A few sprigs of ivy add a rustic touch while the water makes the pebbles glisten and shine appealingly.

seashells and stones

It is a particular pleasure to make a decorative feature for your home that uses materials and objects that you can collect on a visit to the seashore or a day out in the country, or one which employs more exotic items that may be mementos of a vacation abroad. This attractive fountain has a marine theme – it uses seashells, pebbles, and driftwood to create a miniature raised beach in a terracotta bowl over which a softly flowing stream of water plays. One word of warning though – while it is very satisfying to use things found while beachcombing, concerns about the conservation of natural resources and care for the environment mean that certain beauty spots are now protected sites from which material must not be removed. Always check with local regulations and keep an eye open for public warning signs before starting to collect items like pebbles, rocks, or shells to take home.

The central feature of this display is a large shell through which a hole is drilled to allow it to be fitted on to the rubber pipe that runs up from the pump. Shells like this are delicate and may easily shatter if you attempt to drill through them with a power tool. It is safer to use a sharp penknife to make a little indentation in the surface of the shell and then to rotate the blade manually to ream out a hole. Once you have a sufficiently large aperture to work with, you can use a round file to complete the job.

The inside of the terracotta bowl is varnished with a satin varnish to give it a luster that sets off the delicate colors of the shells. Also note that a brick is used to bulk out the space inside – not only does this save on the quantity of decorative stones and shells that you need to fill the bowl, it also means that less water is required in the reservoir and thus saves weight. It is a technique that can be applied to many similar types of water features.

construction

1 *Shells like this are delicate. Make the hole carefully with a blade and then file the edges smooth. Using a power drill might cause it to shatter.*

2 *Sit the pump on a tile and place it on a brick in the bowl. You must fit about 2 in (5 cm) of rubber pipe to the pump so that it extends to the shell.*

3 *Fill the bowl with a selection of pebbles and stones, ideally collected from a beach. These help to hold the pump securely in place.*

4 *Adding seashells helps to create the impression of a rocky beach in the reservoir. The shells and stones also help to take up space and so reduce the volume of water needed.*

5 *Now the shell that acts as the fountainhead can be connected to the rubber tube. The rubber will compress slightly and so form a nice watertight seal.*

A few small shells added to the fountain shell help to disguise the pipe that carries the water up from the pump.

6 The final touch is created by adding a piece of bogwood to the display. This is material that is available from aquarium shops – it is sometimes added as a decoration to fish tanks. Here it gives the impression of a piece of driftwood that has washed up on the shoreline.

17

chinese pavilion

Some new elements and construction techniques are introduced in this feature which draws on Chinese themes to create a display that really comes into its own after dark. First, a light is used to illuminate the little Chinese pavilion that sits next to the gurgling fountain. Such lights are supplied as an integral part of a combined pump and light unit – the light is wired to the pump which plugs into a transformer that is connected to the main socket. The connections are waterproof and they allow you to introduce a light into a water feature safely. Do NOT attempt to use electric lights independently of the pump and transformer – you will risk serious injury.

Second, a bamboo spout is connected directly to the pump outlet. Bamboo is an excellent material to work with. Its rigidity and watertightness make it well suited to small water features. As it is available in all sorts of sizes and diameters, it is relatively easy to find a piece whose inner diameter matches the size of the nozzle on which is to be fixed. In this case, the flow regulator of the pump is operated by twisting its outlet nozzle, so you are able to control the flow of water coming out of the bamboo spout simply by twisting the cane itself. An elegant solution!

This set-up also uses expanded polystyrene (the familiar packaging material) as the base support for the display. The advantage of polystyrene is that it is light, easily cut to create spaces into which the various units will fit snugly, and it displaces a large volume for its mass so you do not need to use gallons of water in the reservoir. Do remember, however, that it floats, so you need to use stones or pebbles in the display to weigh it down.

construction of the pavilion

1 *The roof of the little pavilion is made from four pieces of black card that are slightly curved as shown in the photograph. Temporarily tack the pieces in position with clear adhesive tape.*

2 *The joins of the roof are secured with balsa cement. Once this is dry, a decorative edging stripe can be added with a gold pen and the whole roof is then coated with clear varnish to make it shine.*

3 *The framework for the pavilion is made from stalks of dried corn glued together. The finished example shows how the roof sits on top of this.*

4 *The windows are made from pieces of tracing paper glued into position inside the framework. The symbol on the side is Chinese for "water."*

construction

1 *This piece of bamboo has been chosen because it fits snugly on the pump outlet. Twisting the bamboo serves to open and close the flow regulator on the pump to control the flow rate.*

2 *The pump and light are fitted into a base made of polystyrene that is cut to fit in the bowl. A second length of bamboo which will act as a flower holder is added at the back.*

The combination of light and flowing water works well in this fountain. The tracing paper used for the pavilion windows is opaque so the bulb is hidden from view.

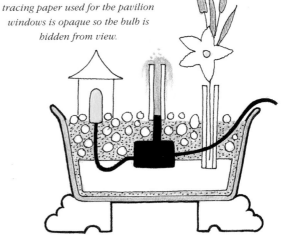

3 *The whole of the polystyrene base is covered with fine gray gravel. This provides a substrate through which the water drains back to the pump. Note how you do not necessarily need large volumes of water to keep a fountain running.*

4 *The floral decoration is made of dried stalks of corn dyed blue and an artificial lily. The glass plate at the back of the display simply rests against a black plate stand.*

bonsai garden

The Oriental theme is further developed in this classic Japanese ensemble which combines a bamboo water spout with a bonsai shrub, a single piece of volcanic rock, some pebbles, and white quartz gravel in a cool and understated way. Contemplation of the quiet running of the water and the simple architecture of the feature will help to induce a mood of calm on even the most stressful day.

Bonsai is the technique of producing extremely dwarf varieties of trees and shrubs by growing them in small pots and by regular careful pruning of the roots to restrict growth. It originated in China but was taken up and developed as an artform in Japan around the 8th century A.D. The plant used here is a variety of *Serissa foetida,* a small, evergreen shrub that is native to the moist, open woodlands of southeast Asia. While

it is a moisture-loving plant that requires watering frequently, remember that no bonsai will tolerate being stood in water, so it is necessary to keep it in a separate container isolated from the water reservoir.

It is important in this feature that the water should tumble accurately out of the bamboo spout onto the runnel that leads to the rock pool. Too strong a flow will result in an arc of water that may even clear the edge of the container! Naturally you can use the pump's own flow regulator to adjust the rate of flow, but subtle "fine-tuning" can also be achieved by introducing small controlled leaks in the plastic piping that runs hidden from view from pump to spout. If you do this, make sure that the hole points inward rather than outward so that the deliberate leak will spout back into the reservoir, not onto the surrounding tabletop.

construction

1 *The reservoir for this fountain is made from a black seed tray. A large piece of polystyrene is placed in the bottom as a filler.*

2 *The spout is made from two pieces of bamboo mitered together (see pages 12-13 for details of how this is done). You must fully insert the inner plastic tube before fixing the 90° joint so that the pipe runs all the way from base to spout.*

3 *The bamboo spout fits to the pump outlet by means of a piece of flexible tube. The unit is then positioned in the bottom of the reservoir and it is held in position by another piece of polystyrene which is wedged into the corner.*

4 *The main piece of rock is then positioned on the base. It is situated beneath the point where the water will run out of the bamboo fountainhead.*

5 *A small bowl acts as a receiving pool. It has a hole in its base so that water can flow back into the reservoir.*

6 *Two stones, held together with mastic, are then placed in the inner pool. Water will splash gently over them.*

7 *Finally a bamboo runnel is positioned and again secured in place with mastic.*

Flow regulation is important for this fountain to work properly. The water must drop into the bamboo runnel. You may need to experiment with a controlled leak to achieve a satisfactory effect.

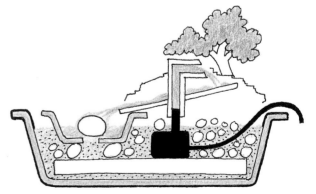

shishi-odoshi

This intriguing creation presents a miniature version of a Japanese *shishi-odoshi* or deer-scarer. These tipping bamboo fountains were originally used by farmers to scare away deer and other wild animals that threatened to eat their young plants and crops. They work like this: a stream of water pours out of a bamboo spout into the mouth of another piece of bamboo that is pivoted and which contains a counterweight at its closed end. As the bamboo fills with water, it grows heavier; eventually the weight of water causes it to tip downward. As a result, the water pours out. Once relieved of this weight, the counterweight at the other end causes the pivoted tipper to rock smartly back to its raised position. As it does so, the weighted end strikes a stone and the resulting "crack" scares away wildlife.

Remember that bamboo saws and drills are good construction tools provided that are sharp. The counterbalance is made by sawing the end off the tipper next to a knuckle joint and filling part of the hollow interior with plasticine. The end can then be relocated and it will be held in place by the plasticine filling. Alternatively you can glue it in position. Make sure that you only drill out part of the entire length of the tipper. The knuckles in the wood are natural barriers that hold back the water, enabling the up-and-down motion. If the whole length of bamboo were to fill with water, it would get stuck in the up position. Also make sure that the cross-piece upon which the tipper pivots is sited behind the knuckle that blanks off the water so that a correct equilibrium in the tilting mechanism can be achieved.

The exact rate of flow is crucial to the regular to-and-fro motion of the *shishi-odoshi,* so be prepared for some trial and error to get this right. The time spent will seem well worthwhile when you sit entranced by the gentle rocking movements of your own deer-scarer.

construction

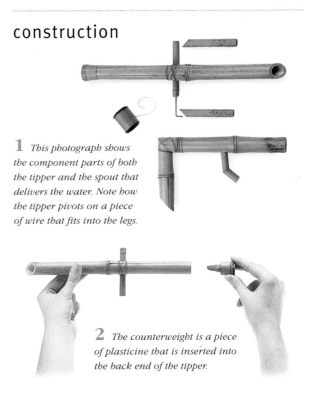

1 *This photograph shows the component parts of both the tipper and the spout that delivers the water. Note how the tipper pivots on a piece of wire that fits into the legs.*

2 *The counterweight is a piece of plasticine that is inserted into the back end of the tipper.*

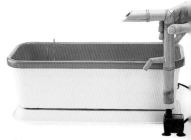

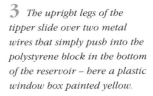

3 *The upright legs of the tipper slide over two metal wires that simply push into the polystyrene block in the bottom of the reservoir – here a plastic window box painted yellow.*

4 *The bamboo spout is attached directly to the pump outlet and the whole pump unit is slotted into an aperture that is cut for it in the polystyrene base.*

5 *Mounting the tipper on the wire supports that were shown in position in picture 3.*

6 *Here the "striker" stone is being placed under the tipper. When the tipper rocks back, it hits the stone and makes a sharp noise.*

7 *Pebbles and gravel are used to adorn the finished fountain. The little inner bowl is painted terracotta.*

The finished shishi-odoshi can be decorated with silk flowers. In this case you do not need to make a hole in the inner bowl – it simply brims over with water. The schematic diagram (right) reveals how the tipper will rock up and down on its pivoted section.

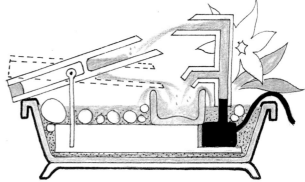

midnight grotto

We saw in the Chinese Pavilion (pages 18-19) how the addition of a light to a tabletop feature can add an intriguing element of mystery. In this Midnight Grotto the principle is taken one step further; the light is situated underwater on the floor of a cave sculpted out of a "rock" headland. Brilliantly colored glass beads are scattered over the base above the light source so that we see light reflected through what appear to be precious jewels hidden underwater.

The "rock" out of which the grotto is sculpted introduces us to a new material – expanding foam-filler. This is a home store material sold in aerosol dispenser cans that is used for filling holes and cavities in masonry. When it is squirted out of the can, it swells up rapidly to occupy a space around three times its original volume. It dries rapidly and can be cut and sanded into any desired shape within about 12 hours. It can also be painted and varnished as appropriate. When you

consider that it is also waterproof, can be easily gouged and channeled to create ducts for the pipework, and is light and portable, it is easy to understand why I recommend foam-filler for features that need to mimic the look of natural rock or stone outcrops.

Once again expanded polystyrene is used as the base in which the pump and light are situated, and the foam-filler rock headland is secured to this by means of long wire pins which hold it securely in place.

construction

1 *The polystyrene base has to be weighed down with stones to prevent it from floating when the reservoir is filled with water.*

2 *Slots are also cut into the polystyrene to accommodate the pump and the light that is attached to it. The bowl has been sprayed with gray paint.*

3 *A long piece of flexible tube runs up from the pump through a channel gouged out of the filler material to emerge in the "roof" of the grotto.*

4 *A small plastic deflector will direct the flow of water downward. The filler is painted with emulsion and then sprayed with car paint.*

5 *The floor of the cave is covered with translucent colored glass beads mixed with a few small seashells. The beads can normally be found in any reasonably well-stocked craft shop.*

6 *As the foam filler material is easy to pierce, it is a simple matter to make holes for the stems of pieces of ivy to decorate the "headland." These also serve to conceal the long wire pins that anchor the filler to the polystyrene base below. Without the pins, the filler would float on the water.*

The effect of the light shining through colored stones as the water trickles down is beautifully conveyed in this photograph of the finished fountain.

7 *Smaller pieces of ivy with less sturdy stems can be attached to the display by means of U-shaped wire staples pressed into the filler.*

25

alpine stream

construction

In tabletop terms, it's just a small step from a rocky headland to an Alpine mountain, and foam-filler is the key. In this dramatic display, this material is again used, but on this occasion the course of a stream is carved out of the surface of the mountain so that water flows from the pump's outlet at the top of the hill down the stream, through a pool dug deep in the rock in which a mister is sited, and then on down the stream to tumble onto the rockwork at the base of the mountain. The course of the stream is coated with fiberglass resin into which small pieces of gravel are set, both to give the effect of a pebble-strewn brook and to seal the watercourse so that the water runs quickly.

Much of the drama and atmosphere of this creation is brought about by the use of a mister which causes skeins of fog to waft eerily out of the hillside and drift down over the rockwork. The mister is a small, electrical device which works by creating ultrasonic waves which vaporize water lying above a transducer plate. Note that the mister has to be completely submerged in water to function properly. Like the lights already mentioned, the mister runs off a transformer which steps down the voltage of the power delivered to the unit. But it runs independently of the pump, so you have to allow for a second electrical cable to run through a channel carved in your mountain.

The mister's pool is formed by the upturned top of an aerosol can which is sunk into a hole cut in the foam mountainside and then sealed in position with a layer of fiberglass resin piped around the lip of the lid to make it watertight. The Alpine flowers and plants which decorate the mountain are simply stems cut from artificial flowers which are pushed into the foam and bent into a convincing position.

1 *The filler material is sold in aerosol spray cans. Remember to wear protective gloves and then spray a quantity into a bowl lined with a polystyrene base. The filler rapidly expands and hardens.*

2 *Once the filler has hardened, it can be cut to shape and a channel for the watercourse carved into it. A hole for the mister reservoir must also be made quite high up on the side of the slope.*

3 *Once the foam block has been carved to the right shape, give it a coat of paint. Brown emulsion has been used here, but the choice is up to you. Green paint is also used to give a stippled effect that mimics the look of vegetation.*

4 *When the paint has dried (this can take some time as the material is not naturally absorbent), feed the plastic pipe attached to the pump up through the channel that you have created so that it emerges at the top of the stream.*

5 *The mister then goes into its reservoir – an upturned aerosol can top sealed in place. The mister must be entirely submerged in water to work properly.*

6 *To decorate the mountainside, try using individual sprigs and flower clusters cut from artificial flowers. The little sprays of blooms look like Alpine plants.*

The wisps of mist drifting out of the mountain cave certainly add a touch of mystery to this unusual fountain.

7 *Complete the display by adding fine washed gravel and a few larger stones to the base of the reservoir. Fill the bowl with water and turn on the pump. Remember that it will take a while for the fountain to prime itself and for the mister reservoir to fill to a sufficient depth.*

desert oasis

This scene of an arid desert in which a single water pump is running to provide relief for parched travelers makes use of a bowl-within-a-bowl to allow us to mix a feature flowing with running water with plants that traditionally grow in areas where water is scarce – cacti. Cacti make use of large barrel-like stems to store water to sustain them over periods of drought, while their leathery skins serve to minimize water loss. Remarkably their spines also shade the plants and help them to collect and absorb water. Naturally such plants do not tolerate exposure to free-flowing water, so they must be isolated from the water source in a tabletop feature such as this. This is achieved by situating a separate bowl containing the water and the pump inside the terracotta bowl that houses the whole feature, and then burying the cacti in their pots in the gravel that is used to fill and dress the surface of the bowl.

The little hand pump is made from a short length of plastic pipe which is cut into two pieces at a 45° angle. These two pieces are then mitered together and stuck with superglue. Another piece is then stuck on at a less acute angle to produce the down-turned spout, and the whole assembly is painted with acrylic paint. This unit is simply connected to the electrical pump's outlet by a short length of rubber tube. If you want to add a handle for further effect, this is easily made out of a piece of wire bent into the appropriate shape and glued to the side of the plastic pipe.

construction

1 *The little hand pump is made from a length of plastic tubing. It is cut at a 45° angle and mitered together with superglue as shown here. The downward angled piece that forms the spout is cut at a less acute angle so that it projects away from the crosspiece.*

2 *This fountain features a bowl-within-a-bowl so that the reservoir of water can be kept separate from the dry bowl containing the cacti. The edge of this dish is disguised by sticking individual pieces of gravel on to a thin layer of mastic run around its rim.*

3 *The central element in the display is this wooden model of a banana tree which is screwed securely to the polystyrene base which sits inside the water reservoir. If you cannot find anything like this, you might consider making an artificial palm tree or a cactus to suit the scene.*

4 *The pump and spout attachment fit snugly into a slot cut in the base next to the banana tree.*

5 *Use stones and a layer of gravel to disguise the pump and the base material in the bowl of the reservoir.*

Running water and desert plants make an eye-catching combination. Remember that natural evaporation will deplete the reservoir, so regular top-ups will be needed.

6 *Complete the display by setting individual pots of cactus into recesses cut into the polystyrene and then filling in around them with gravel and stones. Remember to add water only to the area around the concealed pump.*

mediterranean courtyard

For this evocation of the dazzling white walls of a sun-drenched Mediterranean villa what better than to bring into view the expanded polystyrene material that we have been using up till now as a base? Here it is cut into shapes to represent the walls of a courtyard, and painted with thick white emulsion paint so that a texture is created on the surface which makes it look as if the walls have been hand-rendered. The flower borders to the left and right are simply holes cut out of the polystyrene and decorated with stems cut from artificial plants.

The courtyard area itself appears as if it has been tiled. There are various ways of doing this. You could use actual pieces of tile or mosaic, but you have to be careful to cut and position them accurately to achieve a nice regular pattern. I have used a more forgiving material here – foamboard – which can be cut easily with a penknife. The individual pieces are stuck into position and then grouted. Then the separate tiles are painted with acrylic paint in contrasting shades of blue and, when dry, they are given a coat of clear varnish to make them waterproof. Remember to leave a small gap around the edge of the tiled area so that the water can flow back into the reservoir in the bottom of the bowl.

The standing well is fashioned from a small ceramic bowl. Drill a small hole through it and push in a drinking straw to make the overflow pipe. Then paint the whole unit with terracotta-colored emulsion paint and apply a finishing coat of varnish.

construction

1 *Begin by cutting a circular piece of polystyrene slightly smaller than the circumference of the terracotta dish and position it in the bowl. Three other slabs of polystyrene make the back and side walls of the villa. A hole for the spout is let into the back wall.*

2 *The tiles are made from small pieces of foamboard that are painted in two shades of blue and arranged in a checkerboard pattern. Once in place, the tiles are grouted and then treated with a coat of clear varnish to make them properly waterproof.*

3 *The spout from which the water will pour out of the back wall is made from a short piece of bamboo split in half down the middle to make a* small runnel. *This is pushed all the way through the hole in the back wall. The flexible pipe from the pump outlet connects to this runnel.*

4 *The semicircular roof tiles are made from lengths of plastic tube that are sectioned lengthways and painted with terracotta emulsion paint.*

5 *The pump sits in a slot cut in the polystyrene base. The picture shows how the outlet pipe fits to the bamboo runnel.*

7 *White gravel is also used in the bottom of the little well. This is made from a small pot which has a drinking straw inserted into a hole drilled in its side. Finally, use artificial plant stems to decorate the flower borders cut in the side walls.*

6 *The small gap at the edge down which the water drains back into the bowl is disguised with pieces of white gravel.*

copper and slate waterfall

We are all familiar with the hanging signs that stand outside country hotels and inns tempting the passing traveler to venture inside. This fountain takes its inspiration from such signboards that sway in the wind and rain. It features a piece of slate that is attached by wire hangers to a length of bent copper tubing. The copper tube has a number of holes drilled into it and water is pumped from the copper reservoir through this tube so that it pours down across the face of the slate like a falling curtain of rain. The material used for the pipework is microbore copper tubing which is available from plumber's merchants – it is sometimes used for central heating work. One end of the pipe attaches to the pump, while the other must be blocked so that the water backs up the pipe and is forced to emerge through the drilled holes. The microbore

pipe can easily be bent by hand but you must do this carefully, and work slowly piece by piece, as the metal gets more brittle and liable to snap the more it is handled and worked. About 6.5 ft (2 m) of pipe was needed to make this fountain.

In order to make the water pour nicely across the face of the slate, you will probably need to deflect it forward from the vertical plane slightly. If you do not do this, the water tends to drop past the slate rather than course over it in a regular flow. I have used a deflector made from a piece of foamboard that is attached to a collar fashioned from rigid plastic tubing. Cut a small section out of this collar and then split it longitudinally – this allows you to slide it over the outlet pipe like a sleeve. You can then maneuver it backward and forward to push the slate into the optimum position.

construction

1 *The microbore copper tubing can be bent into shape by hand providing that you work carefully and do not exert too much force. The metal has a tendency to snap if it is bent back and forth too vigorously.*

2 *One you have created the finished curve that you want, drill a series of small holes in the under surface of the upper section of the fountain. Use a small drill bit initially – the holes can always be enlarged later if necessary.*

3 *A small deflector is used to push the slate forward slightly so that it hangs in the curtain of water droplets. It is made from a piece of foamboard that is fitted to a sleeve of tubing that slips over the rigid outlet pipe from the pump.*

4 *Now introduce the copper tube into the bowl. The end that attaches to the pump outlet is padded with tape to ensure a tight fit. The other end must be arranged so that water backs up the copper pipe to the leak holes.*

5 *Add two hangers for the slate. These are pieces of wire bent to shape and crimped on with a pair of pliers. Then add some dark gravel to the bowl.*

6 *A few pieces of volcanic-type rock help to give extra stability to the structure. The color also complements the gray of the gravel and slate.*

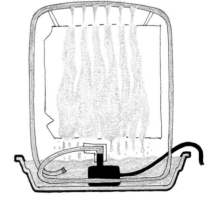

7 *Now hang the piece of slate from the two wire hooks. You may need to experiment with the position of the hooks a little to ensure that the top edge of the slate hangs horizontally.*

8 *This view of the reverse side of the fountain shows how the little deflector works. It can be pushed backward and forward on the outlet pipe until the ideal position is found.*

helter skelter

Now it's time for something a little more ambitious.

We saw in the Alpine Stream (pages 26-27) how a mister can be used to create an unworldly effect, while the light in the Chinese Pavilion (pages 18-19) illustrated how the eye can be encouraged to focus on a specific element in a display. This feature combines both a light and a mister with a helter skelter-like water chute down which the water races before it tumbles into the clouds of fog that hover over the reservoir bowl. This is very atmospheric, and a great visual effect to enliven any nighttime occasion.

The spiral water chute and the roof of the lantern are made from mounting board. It is easy to work with and readily accepts the precise cutting required to fashion the component parts. Remember to use a sharp penknife or craft knife to ensure clean edges. The various elements are assembled with modelling glue – it sticks quickly and securely. Any parts of the design that are going to be directly exposed to water must then be liberally varnished to make them waterproof.

The lantern is very easy to make – it is actually just three pieces of rectangular glass taped along the edges so that they can be folded into a triangular arrangement. The stained glass effect is created by the use of self-adhesive lead strips. This material is sold in home stores. All you need to do is to cut the length you require, peel off the paper backing strip and burnish the lead down into position to create the look of glass panes. The lead can be bent and worked into all sorts of shapes – circular skylights, portholes, curved windows, the choice is yours. The colored patterns are made by painting translucent glass paint onto the individual panes. When illuminated from within, the effect is magical.

construction of the spiral water chute

1 *The water chute is made from pieces of mounting board cut into a spiral shape. Thin pieces of board are then glued to the edges of the spiral to make retaining walls that prevent the water from overflowing.*

2 *The downward twist in the spiral is provided by this L-shaped bracket of mounting board. Stick one end to the underside of the top curve and the other to the underside of the lower curve.*

3 *Add a small lip at the bottom of the chute and then glue the bamboo delivery pipe in place as illustrated. Finish by painting the whole item with terracotta paint and then varnish it liberally.*

construction of the water deflector

1 *This small deflector chute attaches to the side of the fountain. It collects the water as it flows off the end of the helter skelter and channels it into the center of the reservoir bowl.*

2 *It is made from pieces of mounting board to which a slotted fin is fixed as shown. This component is then also painted and varnished to make it waterproof.*

construction of the lantern

1 *The roof of the lantern is made from three triangles of mounting board joined together, and then painted.*

2 *The individual panes of the lantern windows are created by sticking self-adhesive lead strips onto sheets of glass.*

3 *The panes are then painted with different shades of glass paint. Choose colors that suit your room.*

4 *If you use strips of black insulating tape to join the three lantern windows, the pieces hinge together easily.*

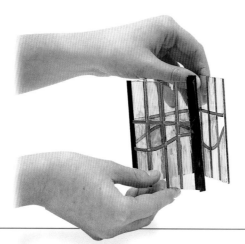

5 *If the pieces of glass are the same width, you will find you have made an equilateral triangle with angles of 60° into which the roof fits snugly.*

6 *This view of the roof shows how the underside is constructed. The small inner triangle fits neatly inside the triangular section made by the three sheets of glass.*

construction

1 *The bowl of the fountain sits on a plinth made from a sturdy cardboard tube. Fins made of foamboard are glued to it and then it is painted.*

2 *The conical bowl in this case is the base of a plastic flower stand which has been inverted. The masking tape ensures a tight fit.*

3 *This view shows the mister already in position and the combined pump and light unit being positioned on a base layer of gravel.*

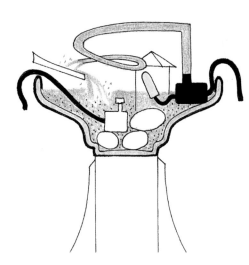

4 *The lantern is then positioned over the light bulb. Note how an extra little support has been taped to the left edge of the lantern. This helps to hold up one side of the helter skelter. Then add some cobbles.*

5 *The whole helter skelter chute then fits onto the pump outlet. The right-hand curve will be supported by the extra strut on the lantern. The final step is to clip the deflector chute onto the edge of the bowl.*

The diagram shows clearly the relative positions of the pump, light, and mister. It is important to sit the deflector chute directly under the lip of the helter skelter.

When the lights are low, this
fountain comes into its own.
The glow of the lantern
through the fog is magical.

Warning:

*Remember not to sit
this fountain on or
near a valuable piece
of furniture. As it is
running, a mister
inevitably causes
splashes and drops of
condensation which
will damge wood and
veneer surfaces.*

The photograph above reveals
how the spiral of the helter
skelter is supported by the strut
that is attached to the side of
the lantern. The deflector
simply slots on to the bowl.

bamboo watersteps

The beauty of water is that it is an infinitely variable medium that responds to our interventions with all kinds of subtle changes of eddy, ebb, and flow. For this bamboo staircase, we want to encourage the water to fan out and descend the stairs like a moving carpet. Rather than relying on a single spout, this is achieved by delivering the water to a bamboo pipe at the top of the feature into which three holes are drilled. A small piece of bamboo is used as a baffle to deflect the flow from these three apertures back toward the staircase. As a result the three jets fan out and intermingle as they bounce back onto the face of the bamboo steps and the water then flows down the individual steps in a wide stream.

The steps that make up the staircase are fashioned from lengths of bamboo that are varnished to give them a deep luster. Each one is held in position by mastic and the joints between the bamboo steps are also filled with mastic. This can be painted with acrylic paint in any color that you like and the whole assembly finished with another coat of varnish to make it thoroughly waterproof. The decorations include artificial bamboo foliage placed in front of the display and a large artificial lily used to create a visual counterpoint to the rounded smoothness of the bamboo steps.

construction

1 *The base of the fountain is made from a rectangle of polystyrene onto which two triangular pieces are pinned.*

2 *Position the first bamboo step on two toothpicks stuck into the polystyrene supports. Make sure it is level.*

3 *Build up the steps one by one, securing them in place with mastic. The top step has three holes drilled in it.*

4 *The water delivery pipe is made from two pieces of bamboo mitered together. This fits directly to the pump outlet.*

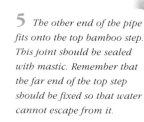

5 *The other end of the pipe fits onto the top bamboo step. This joint should be sealed with mastic. Remember that the far end of the top step should be fixed so that water cannot escape from it.*

6 *Add some heavy rocks to weigh down the polystyrene base to prevent it from floating. Then, add a generous layer of gravel to the container.*

7 *Finally fit the bamboo baffle which deflects the water onto the staircase. The detail shot shows the wire is twisted to prevent the baffle from spinning.*

glowing pyramid

Part of the fascination of moving water lies in the way in which it reflects and refracts the light. This stylish creation combines moving water, reflective glass beads, and two different types of light sources to brilliant effect. As the water trickles down the faces of the pyramid, it is illuminated by candles that can either be set on the "shore" next to the pyramid or floated in the water in the body of the bowl. Tea lights will float naturally in water so you do not need any special contrivances to enjoy these floating features. By using a pump with an integral light fitting attached to it, an electric light can also be sited in the water. This glows through a covering of glass beads poured into the base of the bowl and produces a subtle ambient light that radiates up through the water.

The pyramid itself is made from a sheet of tin, in this case taken from an ordinary roasting pan. Remember that you need only make the two sides of the pyramid that will face into the room – the rear of the feature can be left open to allow access to the pump, provided that the fountain is not situated in a spot where people may walk around it. The blue stones that have such an attractive luster are glass beads that are available in various colors from craft shops. They are slightly flattened rather than being globes, which makes them much easier to attach to the pyramid and its sides. Remember to use a clear adhesive to do this so that the natural brilliance of the glass is not dimmed by opaque glue.

The pyramid sits in two grooves sculpted out of a polystyrene base. A channel is also cut into the base to allow the wire for the light to be countersunk out of the way. It emerges from under the front lip of the pyramid and the light lies on the bottom of the dish. More glass beads are used to cover the bulb and hide it from direct view. The spout out of which the water flows has two holes cut into either side of the exit pipe. This causes the water to flow down both faces of the pyramid simultaneously. You may need to experiment with the flow regulator to achieve a balanced effect – too much pressure will cause a spout rather than the desired gentle trickle.

construction

1 *The reservoir is made from a plastic flower pot saucer sprayed with silver paint. It is mounted on a triangular base made from mounting board.*

2 *The two faces of the pyramid fit into a slot cut in a polystyrene base. The pump and wire for the light are countersunk in a similar way.*

3 *The glass beads that decorate the pyramid's sides are stuck on with clear adhesive. The fact that they are flattened helps them to stick.*

4 *Once the positions of the slots for pyramid and wires have been established, cover the whole of the base with a layer of aluminum foil.*

5 *The exposed edges of the base should also be covered with rows of glass beads in exactly the same way.*

6 *Now put the pyramid into position. It is important that the front apex projects slightly over the polystyrene base to leave room for the wire for the light to pass through.*

The finished fountain combines flickering light and moving water very effectively. The little spout at the top of the fountain head – here concealed by a decorative glass bead – is drilled on either side so that water flows evenly onto both faces of the pyramid.

7 *The pump is stuck to a piece of foamboard to give it stability. The visible part of the pipe is decorated with glitter-effect blue nail polish.*

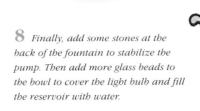

8 *Finally, add some stones at the back of the fountain to stabilize the pump. Then add more glass beads to the bowl to cover the light bulb and fill the reservoir with water.*

scallop shell cascade

In medieval times the scallop shell was an emblem worn by pilgrims on the road to the shrine of St. James in Santiago de Compostela in Spain. Walter Raleigh famously alluded to it in his poem *The Pilgrimage:* "Bring me my scallop shell of quiet, My staff of faith to walk upon." In this display, we echo the beautiful curves and sweeps of this shell to create an elegant fountain down which water trickles in a series of steps. The pipe from which the water tumbles is made from copper bent into a sinuous curve, so that the whole effect is one of grace and proportion.

The process by which the copper pipe is bent to the required U shape is quite simple. A number of cross cuts are made in the pipe with a hacksaw. Make sure that you only cut to a point about halfway through the pipe so that the metal retains enough integrity to avoid it snapping when bent. You should make about 12 such cuts evenly spaced about 0.4 in (1 cm) apart. Then bend the pipe gently by hand so that it curves back on itself like the handle of an umbrella. Next you must make a hole near the base of the pipe through which the flexible tube from the pump can be fed. Again this can be done by making a transverse saw cut and driving in the lower lip with a hammer and metal punch to enlarge the aperture to the required size. The holes for the wire hooks which carry the shells are made by drilling small holes at appropriate points and then easing them out with a screwdriver.

The antique effect is created by spraying the whole fountain – base, stand and shells – with instant verdigris spray paint. It creates a subtle finish that matches the restraint of the overall design. If you want to conjure up a more mysterious atmosphere, it would be quite simple to incorporate a mister into the reservoir bowl so that the shells and pebble decorations appear to rise out of a swirling sea of fog.

construction

1 *The copper pipe can be bent once a series of cuts have been made with a hacksaw partially through one section.*

2 *Make two cuts vertically downward at the other end and then splay the cut pieces into a star shape with pliers.*

3 *Drill holes through the legs of the "star" and screw this onto a wooden base which also will house the pump.*

4 *Each of the shell steps is secured by means of a nut attached to its corner. Drill the hole for the nut using a masonry drill. Take care as the corner may snap.*

5 *The supports are made from a wire hanger bent into shape. Use pliers to tighten the bolt on the nut making sure that you have added a washer to help secure it.*

6 *Once all the components have been assembled, spray them with verdigris spray paint from an aerosol can.*

7 *Then feed flexible tube through the aperture in the copper pipe all the way up and around the curve.*

8 *Each scallop shell is attached via its hanger to the copper pipe. Stagger the holes to create a slight spiral.*

9 *Now attach the pump to the end of the flexible hose that projects from the bottom of the copper pipe.*

10 *The whole fountain sits on a base located in the bottom of a terracotta bowl. Add gravel as ballast.*

11 *Finally, add a selection of seashells to decorate the bowl and to complement the scallop shell steps.*

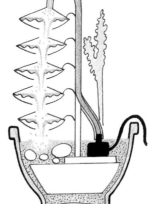

The natural flutings in scallop shells help to contain and channel the water as it flows downward. You will need to angle each shell slightly inward toward the center of the bowl to prevent water from spilling out over the edge onto the tabletop.

fragrant waterfall

This is a very understated arrangement which is pleasing because it is so subtle and restrained. Water trickles out from under a coping stone that sits atop a mound of smooth pebbles, while in the gravel below an aromatic candle flickers. The beauty of this combination of elements is that it appeals to three different senses at once: The eye is stimulated by the juxtaposition of the red candle and red flowers, the ear is soothed by the quiet murmur of the water over the stones, and the nose enjoys the perfume of the candle that fills the air as it burns.

The pebbles that are mounded up to make the waterfall are stuck to one another with mastic, which is an acrylic caulk used for filling jobs by home decorators. Remember to let this dry overnight before you think of turning on the fountain. The mastic will degenerate and lose adhesion if it gets wet before it has properly hardened. The beautiful red lily is an artificial silk flower. It is ideal for the purpose because it will not decay or fade, but it is combustible so take care not to position the candle too close to it or you risk accidentally setting it on fire.

We really want the water to fan out over the width of the pebble falls, so rather than delivering the flow straight out of the end of the plastic pipe, two small nicks are taken out of the sides of the pipe a few millimeters from the outlet to encourage the water to spurt out to the sides. You will need to experiment with your pump setting to get exactly the sort of flow effect that you want, but it is worth persevering as the finished fountain can create a really soothing ambience when it is working at its best.

construction

2 *The pump is positioned at the back of the reservoir bowl and secured in place with more stones. The finished cobble mound will sit in front of it.*

3 *Gray acrylic paint can be applied to the joints between the stones once the mastic has dried to conceal the adhesive and help to blend all the tones.*

4 *The aromatic candle is glued to a stone which is again secured in position on the bottom of the dish with mastic. Take care when using lighted candles in a display. Don't leave a flame unattended.*

1 *The pebble mound is made from individual stones piled on top of one another and held in position with mastic. A polystyrene support structure is positioned behind to give added stability. A small piece of bamboo pipe is also let into this polystyrene backboard – this acts as a flower holder for the artificial lily.*

5 *Decorate the base of the reservoir and all around the candle with fine shingle.*

6 *Add the coping stone to the top of the pile. Note how this conceals the outlet pipe which runs up from the pump.*

This fountain plays on the quieter notes of the scale. The water just leaks softly over the stones as the candle burns. It is ideal for inducing a mood of peaceful contemplation.

7 *Finally, position the artificial flower in its bamboo holder, making sure that the material is kept well away from the candle flame. The bold splash of color lifts the whole display.*

water wheel

Many of the techniques that have been introduced in the previous pages come together in this ambitious fountain – we are going to create a water wheel that spins when the water hits it, a millhouse that is illuminated from within, and below which sits a millpond on which floats a small boat by a jetty. It may sound impossibly difficult, but all that is required is the application of skills that you have already learned and some care and patience when it comes to cutting out and assembling the component parts.

Two basic materials are used. The headland on which the millhouse sits is made of foam-filler in exactly the same way as the mountain was made for the Alpine Stream (see pages 26-27). This can be quite easily cut to shape and a channel excavated to accommodate the bulb and wire of the lamp that lights up the building. The millhouse, water wheel, boat and jetty are all made from foamboard, the same stuff that was used to create the mosaic tiles for the Mediterranean Courtyard (see

pages 30-31). It is good material to work with – it cuts easily and accurately, it is light but rigid enough to hold a shape securely, and it is waterproof when treated with varnish. The slight springiness in texture that is a characteristic of the foam core allows you to fit pieces snugly together as the board will compress a little when it is eased into grooves and joints are cut for it. This is especially useful when assembling the wheel as the unit needs to fit together securely and not sag or move laterally when it starts to turn.

Regulation of the water flow is critical for this feature to work satisfactorily. Too much water and the wheel will spin as if possessed; too little and it will either not move or just idle around listlessly. This fountain uses the small sleeve-like collar shown in the photograph fitted as a flow valve on the delivery pipe. It can be rotated to open or close a hole cut into the tube. In this way a controlled leak is used to fine-tune the water flow allowing the wheel to turn just as you want it to.

construction

1 *The water wheel itself is made from two circles of foamboard mounted on an axle. Cut out twelve segments around the circumference, like the hours on a clock face, and then trim out the inner triangular sections to form the spokes.*

2 *Make two identical circles and mount them on an axle made from a piece of thin plastic tube. The blades of the water wheel are made from narrow rectangular struts of foamboard that slot into the apertures that you have cut around the edges.*

3 *The next element to construct is the millhouse. Again it is made from pieces of foamboard stuck together with modeling glue. The holes for the windows can be cut very easily in the board with a penknife or sharp craft knife.*

4 The roof is made from pieces of corrugated cardboard painted with terracotta emulsion paint. Trim them to the dimensions you require and glue them to the walls of the millhouse.

5 Next comes the jetty. Begin this by cutting a rectangular piece of foamboard for the base and then stick four upright legs or piers to it. Diagonal bracing struts add rigidity to the structure.

6 The deck of the jetty is made from individual "planks" of foamboard stuck to a simple subframe. Foamboard is good material to work with as it light and rigid, and easy to cut into precise shapes.

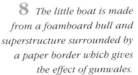

7 When complete, stick the deck of the jetty onto the support piers and leave time for all the adhesive to dry thoroughly.

8 The little boat is made from a foamboard hull and superstructure surrounded by a paper border which gives the effect of gunwales.

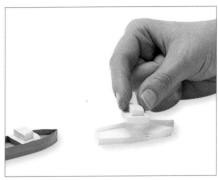

9 The base on which the headland sits is sculpted from a piece of polystyrene which fits inside the plastic seed tray that forms the reservoir. Three large stones are countersunk into it to weigh it down.

10 The headland is made from foam filler in the same way as the Alpine mountain shown on pages 26-27. Once you have formed a satisfactory shape, paint it with white masonry paint to add texture.

11 The headland is then secured to the base by means of long pins fashioned from thin wire. Note how a deep section has been cut into the front of it – this will accommodate the water wheel.

12 *Behind the scenes an aperture has been cut in the foam filler to house the pump and a channel gouged out through which the light is fed.*

13 *The light emerges through the top surface of the headland which has been flattened so that the millhouse will fit squarely on top of it.*

14 *Flow rate is critical to the operation of the water wheel; this detail shows how a shutter valve is incorporated to regulate a controlled leak in the water delivery pipe.*

15 *The pipe runs from the pump through the back of the millhouse and emerges through a front window.*

16 *Then the wheel can be positioned. One end of the axle sits in a little depression under the house, the other is pinned with a wire staple to the foam.*

17 *The jetty sits on the floor of the tray. The water here will form a substantial pool. Both jetty and wheel have been painted with brown emulsion paint and then varnished with gloss varnish for a waterproof finish.*

18 *Fill in around the base of the jetty with some dark gravel. Some of this can be mounded up at one corner of the tray to give the impression of a stony beach. Add larger rocks to complete the effect.*

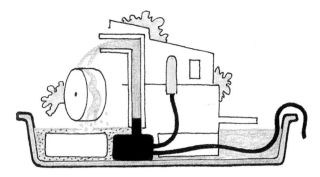

The water wheel in action. This is quite a complicated set-up, but when the wheel starts to turn, it all seems worth it!

19 As a final touch, stick some sprigs of Scandinavian moss to the headland with mastic, and conceal the polystyrene base material with a layer of white gravel.

floating garden

Most of the fountains featured in this book do not draw attention to the water that is contained in the reservoir of the bowl. We have tended to use pebbles, rocks, and gravel as decoration for the bowl so that water appears as if by magic out of a spout or pipe without any indication of where it is held. In this floating garden, however, the reservoir water becomes an integral part of the display as it is used to make a small pool on which lilypads are floated. The surface of the water also reflects the flames of the candles to create a peaceful scene combining soft lights, the gentle sound of tumbling water, and the drift of flowers around the pool. Perfect for a quiet corner of your house or conservatory.

The spout which delivers the water is made from a piece of bamboo. Here the bore of the bamboo exactly matches the gauge of the delivery pipe from the submersible pump so no internal tubing is required – the bamboo fits directly on the pump. The cross pieces are made from pieces of plastic tube mitered together and fitted into holes drilled in the sides of the bamboo. They are painted to match the color of the wood and then the whole spout is varnished. Take care when regulating the flow of this feature. You want to achieve a nice regular flow, but not a torrent that causes a lot of turbulence in the water that will wash the lilypads to the sides of the bowl and cause splashes.

The lilypads are made from foamboard treated with varnish. This material is light, easy to cut, and of course floats on water. You could also use cork. The flowers are artificial silk blooms stuck to the center of the pads with glue. Another attractive option would be to float tea lights on the water.

construction

1 *The lilypads are small circles of foamboard that are cut out with a penknife. Treat each piece with varnish to make it thoroughly waterproof. If you use cork, you do not need to apply any finish.*

2 *Each lily bloom is a silk artificial flower. These are far more durable than real flowers which would fade in hours. Cut a small hole in the middle of each pad and secure the center of the lily with glue.*

3 *The spout is made from a piece of bamboo that is of the right size to fit directly on to the pump outlet. The cross pieces are smaller bore plastic pipe mitered together and painted to match the bamboo.*

4 *To complete the effect, varnish the plastic cross pieces and the bamboo to make them shine, and then attach a few stems of the artificial lilies to the upright using thin wire to hold them in position.*

5 *The pump sits on the bottom of the bowl. Use a tile or piece of foamboard to prop up its unsupported side.*

6 *Connect the bamboo spout to the pump outlet and twist it into place when you are happy with its position.*

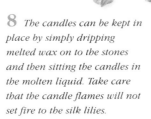

7 *Partially fill the bowl with gravel and add some larger pieces of rock for visual effect. Be careful to avoid getting small pieces of gravel near the pump's inlet; if they get sucked in, they will block the flow.*

8 *The candles can be kept in place by simply dripping melted wax on to the stones and then sitting the candles in the molten liquid. Take care that the candle flames will not set fire to the silk lilies.*

The symmetry of the two jets of water, the two flames reflected in the surface of the pool, and the two floating lilies makes a beautifully balanced effect.

double bubble

This abstract modern tabletop feature turns everything we have learned so far on its head! Normally a successful fountain design requires you to make an attractive and balanced-looking display while hiding all the pipes and the working parts from view. The pleasure for the onlooker comes from watching a stream of water issuing from a spout or fountain and meandering down over the elements of the display. On this occasion the pipework *is* the display. Observers cannot see where the liquid is coming from nor where it is going, but what they can see is a dazzling effect of differently colored water in motion, pulsing and flickering like the blood supply of some surreal being.

The analogy of blood circulation is not as fanciful as it may sound, because the secret of this feature is that it contains two independent reservoirs, similar to the left and right chambers of the heart, and that it is powered by two pumps. The two reservoirs here are teflon-coated baking pans for bread. Each contains a pump linked to a wild jumble of clear pipe that carries liquid from the reservoir and returns it back again to the same receptacle. Each chamber holds water that is dyed with food coloring, so you must take care to connect the return pipes to the correct supply unit or the two colors will gradually mix.

So far, so good. But if you simply use colored water, no texture or light and dark patches will be apparent in the flow and so the tubes will just look static. The trick is to add to each reservoir another liquid that does not mix with water so that the color pattern is broken as the two liquids course through the pipes together; aromatherapy oils are a good choice as they have a pleasant fragrance. Now oil floats on water, so you are faced with the problem of how to ensure that the pumps take a mixture from both the top and bottom of the pans at the same time. The answer is to turn them sideways so that the inlet apertures are partially immersed in the water and partially in the oil. That way both liquids are ingested as the pumps run and they create a dappled, uneven pattern as they flow though the pipes. Once back in the reservoirs, they settle back to their respective levels. It's quite difficult to set up precisely so remember to concentrate on getting the depth of the colored water right first, as the oil simply sits on top of that. But the time taken doing this is worth it – once the fountain is working properly, the effect is wild!

construction

1 *The base of the unit that conceals the two reservoir chambers is made from pieces of mounting board.*

2 *A shallow plinth made from sections of board set at an angle to the base helps to soften the outline.*

3 *Apertures for the in and out pipes and the electrical wires from the two pumps must be cut in the top.*

4 *Now stick the top in position. Note that the back of the structure remains open so that it can slide over the pans.*

5 *Paint the whole base unit with matte blackboard paint and then stick square mirror tiles to the top surface. Varnish all the exposed areas of black paint.*

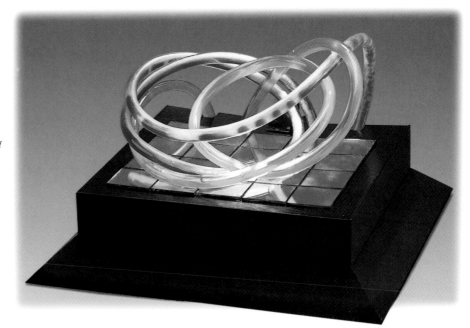

6 *The two reservoirs are oblong baking pans set side-by-side on a baseboard. They can be stuck in place with a layer of decorator's mastic.*

This fountain works best if it is illuminated from above so that the liquids glow in the pipes and light bounces back from the mirror tiles which also reflect the pipework above them.

7 *Now position the two pumps sideways – one in each pan. The pumps are set this way up so that they will take liquid from the two separate layers of water and oil that sit in each pan.*

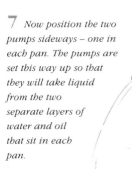

8 *Connect the two knots of transparent pipe to the pumps and stick them together where pipes cross to hold the arrangement in position.*

9 *Make sure that the return pipe is connected to the same reservoir as its outlet so that the colored liquids flow back to the correct reservoirs.*

copper cascade

The modern theme introduced in Double Bubble on the previous pages is continued here with the construction of a steeply angled tower, rather like a thin shark's fin curving up from the tabletop. This serves as the structure on which a raked series of bowls are arranged in the manner of the treads of a ladder. Water is pumped from the bottom sump right to the top of the tower where it flows out into a small copper-colored dish. This has a pipe let into its front edge and the water flows out through this into a second copper dish and so on down the steps of the ladder to the bottom where it pours onto a deflector that channels it back to the sump.

The bowls are made from plastic flower pot saucers sprayed with copper paint. An acrylic-based auto touch-up spray paint was used to do this. Don't use cellulose-based products as they tend to bubble and not give the smooth metallic effect that you want. Each

bowl sits on a horizontal board slat that slides into the tower unit. The slats are fitted with "daggerboards," rather like those found on sailing boats, which press against vertical bracing supports that run across the tower structure – these prevent the bowls from dipping when they become heavy with the weight of accumulated water. The saucers are each drilled and fitted with a short length of rigid plastic pipe which serves as the outflow. The pipe is fixed into position with superglue which is both durable and watertight.

As the pump has to power quite a high "lift," it can take some time for the water to start flowing at a satisfactory rate. It is tempting to fill up each bowl manually to speed up the process, but remember that when you turn off the pump, all the water will eventually drain back into the bottom reservoir. If you have been a bit too generous with your priming, you risk an overflow onto the tabletop.

construction

1 *The tower structure is made from mounting board. The two fin-shaped sides are glued to the base as shown here and then they are stuck together at the top.*

2 *This support structure adds rigidity to the tower at its base and serves to keep the two sides the correct distance apart. The individual copper bowls will slide into the gap.*

3 *This photograph shows details of the internal construction of the tower. The vertical bracing pieces help to hold the copper bowls securely in position.*

4 *The saucers are positioned on slats of mounting board to which vertical fins are added. These prevent the saucers from sagging downward when they fill up with water.*

5 *Drill a hole in the front of each saucer and attach a short plastic spout with superglue.*

6 *The pipe that fits on to the pump is fed through a hole in the side of the tower.*

7 *The pipework is clipped to the side of the tower with little brackets made from cardboard. It attaches to the outlet nozzle at the top. Note how the wire also passes through the hole made for the pipe.*

8 *This unit acts a deflector to channel the water back into the reservoir bowl. The cover section serves to hide the pump in the bottom of the bowl.*

9 *As this deflector unit will be directly exposed to water, remember to coat it liberally with varnish to protect it.*

10 *Spray the individual bowls with bronze or copper paint and, when dry, slide them into position. Fill the reservoir with water and switch on.*

seashell shower

The Scallop Shell Cascade on pages 42-43 showed how you can use natural objects like seashells to produce a stepped waterfall. Here the idea is quite literally turned on its head. A scallop shell is again the centerpiece of the display but this time it is inverted and the water is directed up into the dome of the shell which acts like a canopy. The scallop shell has a series of fluted channels on its inner surface, and by experimenting with the flow of water from the pump you can encourage the water to fan out across the inside of the shell and then to drop in a number of rivulets from its front edge. As you can see in the detail picture of the shell, I have used a curved piece of metal attached to its inner surface to act as a deflector to make the water spread out as it emerges from the outlet pipe. This is important to achieve a nice fan pattern in the flow.

This theme is picked up in the design of the upper reservoir bowl. Three pieces of rigid plastic pipe are attached to the dish in the same way as the individual steps of the Copper Cascade were made (see pages 54-55) to provide a triple outfall into the lower reservoir. The effect of the water cascading from the shell, being collected in the upper dish, only to pour out again in a fan of spouts is fun visually, while the sound of the water adds to the overall effect. One word of warning: Naturally this fountain produces splashes and drops of water may escape from the container; take care when positioning it on a piece of furniture as unwanted splashes may damage the finish of polished wood or lacquered surfaces.

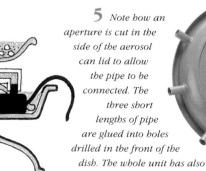

construction

1 *The base of the fountain is made from a flower pot saucer set on top of a pot stand. Both elements are sprayed green.*

2 *Another plastic dish, also sprayed green, is inverted and glued in place in the middle of the reservoir bowl.*

3 *An aperture has been cut with a sharp backsaw in this upturned dish to allow room for the pump to be positioned.*

4 *A feed pipe runs through center of the top dish which is glued to the top of an aerosol spray can.*

5 *Note how an aperture is cut in the side of the aerosol can lid to allow the pipe to be connected. The three short lengths of pipe are glued into holes drilled in the front of the dish. The whole unit has also been sprayed green.*

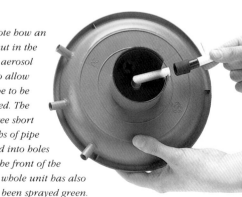

6 *This photograph shows details of how the pipe is attached to the scallop shell. A small tin deflector, glued in with epoxy resin, helps the water to fan out over the shell.*

7 *The scallop shell fountain head then connects to the pipe that runs up through the top bowl (see 4). Note how the shell is set at an angle on its pipe – this helps guide the water into the bowl beneath.*

8 *The assembled top unit is then positioned on the inverted dish in the reservoir. It must be glued in place with waterproof adhesive. The photograph shows how the pipe runs from the concealed pump through the can lid and up to the shell.*

You will need to experiment with the pump setting to get an even flow like this – too strong a jet of water will lead to unwanted splashes.

9 *Both the reservoir bowl and the upper bowl can be decorated with a mixture of gravel and seashells. Take care not to put the gravel too close to the pump inlet – if it sucks in a small stone, it may get blocked.*

candlewall canals

The intriguing feature of this fountain is that running water and lighted candles are combined in close proximity so that the two elements of fire and water unite to create the overall effect. The addition of an electric lamp in the glass bowl means that the display will glow with an atmospheric "subterranean" light while the individual candles flicker on their stands. This is a tabletop feature that really comes into its own after dark.

The wall on which the candles and the waterways are mounted is made of stiff mounting board which can be cut into precise shapes using a penknife or craft knife and a metal ruler. Remember to do this on a cutting mat or piece of discarded board to protect worktops and tables from unwanted cuts. The wall unit can then be painted and varnished to make it watertight. You could of course use other materials for the wall – wood and perspex are alternatives – but remember that it is made from a number of individual elements that have to be cut out accurately, so ease of manufacture is a consideration when choosing your materials.

It is important when crafting the individual candle stands to make them progressively longer as you move down the wall. In this way the candles will be staggered vertically (i.e. the lower ones will project further from the wall that the upper ones) and so the flames of the lights below will not heat up and scorch the stands of the ones above. It is also a good idea to mask the lower surfaces of the stands with aluminum foil before you paint and varnish the unit to ensure that they are thoroughly heatproof. As always when using candles, take care not to leave them unattended when they are burning, stand the unit out of drafts, and be careful when touching the tea lights after they have been lit – the metal casing may still be hot.

construction

1 *Each candle sits on a little step made out of mounting board. The triangular support fins need to be cut at an angle because the wall itself leans back away from the vertical.*

2 *The canal runways of this fountain are also made of mounting board. Mark out the positions for these canals on the back wall before you start to glue pieces in place.*

3 *The candle stands should get progressively longer as you move down the wall so that the candles below do not scorch the bottoms of the steps that are situated above them.*

4 *This little baffle conceals the hole through which the pipe delivers water. Note how the water runways have facing pieces that will channel the water as it flows down.*

5 Once the wall has been constructed, it should be glued to the support structure that holds it up. Note how it leans back away from the vertical plane.

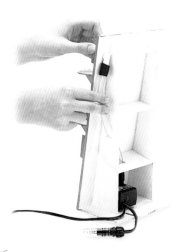

6 Once the wall has been painted and varnished to make it waterproof, the pump and pipework can be attached. The light will simply lie in the reservoir bowl and be covered with white gravel.

7 Set the whole unit in a glass bowl and fill it with white gravel. As a final decorative touch, a couple of lengths of bamboo can be used as holders for sprays of artificial foliage.

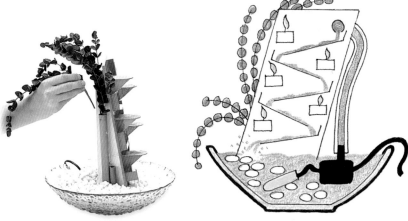

miniature wall mask

This attractive feature takes its inspiration from the spouting mask wall fountains that you often see in formal gardens or on the sides of important buildings in towns and cities. Often these have a very traditional appearance as they use heraldic devices, such as lion's or ram's heads, or masks of classical deities like Apollo, as the decorative centerpiece of the display. Here we want a more modern, stylized effect – the white face surrounded by blue and red flowers has an Art Deco look that conjures up the spirit of the early years of the 20th century.

The face that is featured in these pictures is a plaster mask that was created from a hollow mould which in turn was made by covering the head of a dressmaker's mannequin in plaster bandages treated with a hardening agent. But you don't need to go to these lengths. It is easy enough to buy a face made of polystyrene or papier mâché from craft shops or to use a party mask or even a theatrical prop. It just needs to

be sprayed with white paint to achieve the effect shown. The backing material for the "wall" is polystyrene; this is good to work with as it is very easy to stick the stalks of the artificial flowers directly into the backing board to secure them in place. But any nonabsorbent material would do just as well – plastic, stone, or metal are other options.

A different method of regulating the water flow is shown in this feature. As the wall on which the face is mounted serves to conceal the workings of the fountain, the flexible pipework remains readily accessible for adjustment. So if you need to reduce the flow rate to prevent the spout from firing over the edge of the bowl, just use a small bulldog clip to constrict the pipe. Simple and effective.

construction

1 *Once you have made or bought a suitable mask, paint it white and then attach it to the polystyrene backing board with adhesive or mastic.*

2 *Next drill or bore a hole though the mouth and backboard and thread a length of flexible plastic tube through the aperture you have made.*

3 *A decorative head of "hair" can be created with artificial flowers. Make pilot holes for the stems so that the wires do not bend when pushed in.*

4 *Behind the scenes, the pump simply attaches to the plastic tube. The beauty of this arrangement is that the backboard hides the plumbing.*

5 *The whole fountain stands in a deep plastic pot. Add some large pebbles in the base to give it stability.*

6 *Sit the mask and backboard in position and then add more rocks to fill up the reservoir.*

7 *If you need to restrict the flow of water to prevent splashes, it is easy to attach a bulldog clip to the pipe to cut down the flow rate.*

tipping beak fountain

For the final tabletop feature in the book, I have taken the tipping principle that was introduced in the *Shishi-Odoshi* deer-scarer (pages 22-23) and combined it with a more complex design of a standing bird. The result is that the bird's beak gradually fills with water and then, at the critical moment, it drops open and spills its load into the reservoir below. A counterweight then causes the beak to snap shut and the process starts all over again. It is strangely hypnotic to watch this stylized creature moving seemingly of its own volition in front of your eyes.

Although it may look complicated to make, the basic principle is very simple. A pump drives water up the bird's vertical standing leg. This is channeled through a pipe that is hidden by the bodywork to an outlet in the bird's head. Here the water drips into a hinged beak. When the lower part of the beak is heavy enough, it tips open and spills the water into the reservoir bowl. The counterweight is actually a piece of plasticine attached to one of the side crests that decorate the head, and this is what causes the empty beak to snap shut again once the weight of the water has been released.

The most difficult part of the construction is the assembly of the bird's body which requires patient work. It is made from silver card that is stuck together around a basic skeleton of foamboard bracing pieces. Look at the close-up photographs of the component sections and the internal details closely. The pictures reveal clearly how it all goes together. The tipping mechanism is, of course, the key to this feature, so you may need to experiment by trial and error with the placement and size of the counterweight. The beak needs some fine tuning to work at a satisfactory regular pace. Take care where you position your bird. Inevitably some splashes will occur which may damage surrounding furniture.

construction

1 *This photograph shows the component parts from which the bird is made and details of the internal construction.*

2 *The lower beak is made from waterproofed mounting board. It needs to be durable and relatively heavy.*

3 *The close-up shows how pieces of foamboard act as internal braces to give the body rigidity. The top and sides are held together by little tabs secured with double-sided tape.*

4 *The pipe from the pump extends from the top of the standing leg through the body to the head section of the bird.*

5 *The wings are held in position by small pins that can be driven straight into the foamboard bracing pieces to hold them firmly in place.*

6 *The leg is made from rigid pipe sprayed silver. It fits directly to the pump outlet. The foot is made from pieces of wire.*

The addition of a light shining up through a mound of glass beads adds a final touch of drama to this very pleasing fountain.

7 *The lower beak is held on with a toothpick that fits in a small pipe pushed into the foamboard. A counterweight is stuck to the inside of the crest.*

8 *Sit the fountain in a metal baking tray. Add a piece of pipe as a flower holder and fill the reservoir with a mixture of rocks, beads, and gravel.*

index

Note: *Italic numbers
indicate references to
picture captions*

aromatherapy oils 6, 52

ballast 13, *13, 43*
balsa cement *18*
bamboo 6, *10*, 11, *12,* 12,
  13, 18, *19,* 20, *20, 21,* 22,
  22, 30, 31, 34, 38-39, *38,
  39, 44, 45,* 50, *50, 51, 59*
bogwood *17*
bonsai 20

cacti 28-29, *29*
candles 6, 11, 40, 44, *44, 45,*
  50, *51,* 58-59, *58*
cardboard *18, 36, 47*
cobbles *36*
controlled leaks 12, 13, *13,*
  20, *21,* 46
cork 50, *50*
corn stalks *18, 19*

deer-scarers 6, 22; *see also
  Shishi-Odoshi*
driftwood 16, *17*

electricity safety 9, 18

fiberglass resin 26
flower holder *19, 44, 45, 63*

flowers, artificial 11, *19, 22,*
  26, *27,* 30, *31,* 38, 44,*44,
  45,* 50, *50, 51,* 60, *60*
flow regulators 13, 18, *19,*
  20
foamboard 11, *11,* 30, *30,*
  32, *32, 36, 41,* 46, *46, 47,*
  50, *50, 51,* 62, *62, 63*
foam-filler, expanding 24,
  25, 26, *26,* 46, *47, 48*
foggers *see* misters
foliage, artificial *11, 15, 25,
  31,* 38, *59*

glass 34, *35*
glass beads 11, 24, *25,* 40,
  40, 41, 63
gold thread *12*
gravel 11, *11, 15, 19,* 20,*22,
  26, 27,* 28, *28, 29, 31, 33,
  36, 39, 43,* 48, *49,* 50, *51,
  57, 59, 63*
grouting 30, *30*

lead strips 34, *35*
lights 6, 14, 18, 34, *36, 37,
  41,* 46, *48, 53,* 58, *63*
  halogen 8-9
  underwater 24, 40

mag-drive motors 8
mastic *21, 28,* 38, *38,* 44, *44,
  49, 53, 60*

misters 6, *6,* 8, 9, *9,* 14, 26,
  26, 27, 34, *36, 37,* 42
miter joints *12,* 13, *20,* 28,
  38, 50
mosaic 30
moss, Scandinavian *49*
mounting board 11, *11,* 34,
  34, 35, 40, 52, 54, 58, *58,
  62*

paint, acrylic 28, 30, 39, *44*
  blackboard *53*
  emulsion *24, 26,* 30, *31,
  47, 48*
  glass 34, *35*
  masonry *47*
  spray 10, *24,* 40, *42, 43,*
  54, *55, 56,* 60, *63*
paper, tracing *18, 19*
pebbles *11,* 14, *15,* 16, *16,*
  18, 20, *22,* 42, 44, *44,* 50,
  61
pipework 10, *10,* 12, 13, 14,
  52, *55, 56-57*
piping, copper *10,* 11, 32,
  32, 42, *42, 43*
  plastic 10-11, *10, 12, 14,
  15,* 20, *20, 26,* 28, *28, 31,*
  32, *43, 44, 46,* 50, *50,* 52,
  53, 54, 56, *60*
  rubber *14,* 16, *16,* 28
polystyrene 11, *11,* 13, *13,*
  18, *19,* 20, *22,* 24, *24, 25,*

  26, 28, 29, 30, *30, 31, 38,
  39,* 40, *40, 41, 44, 47, 49,*
  60, *60*
pump cleaning 8
pump technology 8, *8, 9*

reservoir choices 10, *10*
rocks 11, 20, *20, 33, 39,* 48,
  50, *51, 61, 63*

sealant, silicone 10, *14*
shells 16-17, *16, 17, 25,* 42-
  43, *42, 43,* 56-57, *57*
Shishi-Odoshi 12, 22-23,
  62
shutter valve 13, *13, 48*
slate 32-33, *33*
stones 6, 11, *11,* 13, *13,* 16,
  16, 18, *21, 22,* 24, *27, 29,
  41,* 44, *44, 45,* 47

tea lights 11, 40, 50
terracotta 10, 14-15, 16, *43*
tiles 30, *30, 31, 51*
  mirror *53*
trees, artificial 28
tubing *see* pipes

varnish 16, *18,* 24, 30, *30,*
  34, *34, 35,* 39, *48,* 50, *50,
  53, 55,* 58, *59*

water wheels 6, 46-47